BATS

BATS

by Phyllis J. Perry

The Amazing Upside-downers

A First Book

Franklin Watts A Division of Grolier Publishing
New York • London • Hong Kong • Sydney • Danbury, Connecticut

For Casey who is also amazing

*Special thanks to Dr. Nancy B. Simmons,
Assistant Curator of Mammology at the
American Museum of Natural History,
for her helpful comments.*

Photographs ©: BCI: 57 (Karen Marks); Merlin D. Tuttle: 11, 26, 35, 52; Photo Researchers: 18, 22, 45, 48 (Stephen Dalton), 28 (Gregory G. Dimijian), 12 (Roy P. Fontaine), cover (Gilbert S. Grant), 9 (R. Konig Jacana), 2,3 (Stephen Krasemann), 6,50 (Tom McHugh), 14, 19, 24, 33, 36, 42, 40, 43, 46 (Merlin D. Tuttle/Bat Conservation International); Superstock, Inc.: 16; Visuals Unlimited: 29 (James Beveridge), 49 (Thomas Gula), 38 (Joe McDonald), 21 (Science VU), 31 (Richard Thom).

Visit Franklin Watts on the Internet at: http://publishing.grolier.com

Library of Congress Cataloging-in-Publication Data

Perry, Phyllis Jean
    Bats: the amazing upside-downers / Phyllis J. Perry
    p.   cm. — (A First book)
    Includes bibliographical references and index.
    Summary: Discusses the evolution, physiology, conservation, habits, and habitats of the only mammals that fly.
    ISBN 0-531-20342-5 (lib bdg.)   0-531-15903-5 (pbk.)
    1. Bats—Juvenile literature. [1. Bats.] I. Title. II. Series.
QL737.C5P37   1998
599.4—dc21   97-4048
                                                      CIP
                                                      AC

Contents

Egyptian fruit bats hang from the roof of a building during the day.
At dusk, they leave to search for food.

Introducing the Bat 1

As night falls, many animals curl up in burrows, dens, and barns to sleep. But not all animals are ready for rest at the end of the day. Owls, frogs, crickets, raccoons, and many other *nocturnal* animals are just beginning their activities.

In an old abandoned building, hundreds of bats have been quietly hanging upside-down all day long. As the sun begins to set, the bats start to stir. At first, just one or two bats open their eyes. Soon, several are carefully grooming themselves with one foot while continuing to hang by the other. Using their teeth and claws, the bats comb their fur to remove parasites and dirt, shifting their bodies from one awkward position to another. When their grooming is finished, the bats lick their claws clean. They also clean their wings by licking them.

Finally, one bat drops down and flies out through a hole above the rafters. Others quickly follow. The stream of bats explodes out of the building's broken, shingled roof. The bats have burst out into the night in search of food.

BATS AND BIRDS

Because bats can fly, they are sometimes confused with birds. There are well over 9,000 *species* of birds, but only about 950 species of bats. The oldest bird fossils date back about 140 million years. A fossil of the first known bat, found in the shale bed of a shallow lake in Wyoming, is only about 60 million years old. Based on these fossils, it seems that birds and bats *evolved* at different times and had different ancestors. While birds evolved from reptiles, bats' ancestors were shrewlike *mammals* that lived in trees and ate insects.

All birds have certain physical traits in common. Their bodies are covered with feathers, they have beaks, and they lay eggs. Bats share a number of characteristics, too. Their bodies are covered with fur and their wings are covered with smooth skin. They all have teeth and jaws and give birth to live young.

This is the oldest bat fossil ever found. It lived about 60 million years ago.

Bats are the second most diverse group of mammals. (The rodents, which include rabbits, hares, gophers, prairie dogs, muskrats, beavers, porcupines, squirrels, chipmunks, mice, and rats, are first.) Bats account for nearly one-fourth of all the world's mammal species. Bats are found in every part of the world except the Arctic and Antarctic.

BATS AND HUMANS

Bats have always fascinated people. Stories and myths passed down from the most ancient human civilizations mention bats.

The fruit bat, which is still common in Egypt, is pictured in a 4,000-year-old wall painting in an Egyptian tomb. The Mayans of Central America and Mexico worshiped a god who lived under the Earth. This god had the body of a man and the head and wings of a bat. Some Romans thought that wicked people were turned into bats as punishment.

For the Chinese, however, bats are a symbol of good luck. An ancient Chinese design shows five bats with their wings outspread in a circle around a tree. This design is a symbol of happiness, health, wealth, long life, and tranquility.

Today, bats often appear in comic books and movies. Batman is a dark, mysterious figure who strikes fear into the hearts of criminals. And the legend of Count Dracula, the famous vampire from Transylvania, is enough to cause people to lock their bedroom windows at night!

In China, where bats are a symbol of good luck, they are pictured in many designs such as on this cushion from a Buddhist shrine.

Many of the myths and fears associated with bats in the past are still with us today. As a result, most people don't like bats. There is really no reason to fear bats. In fact, they are helpful in many ways. Some bats help plants by scattering their seeds and carrying *pollen* from one flower to another. Others eat insects that would destroy crops.

No, you're not looking at a pig. It's a common Jamaican flower bat.

THE BAT BODY 2

Bats come in many sizes and colors. Some have very strange-looking heads and oddly shaped noses. Some look like tiny dogs or foxes. The snout and silky, silvery fur of a Jamaican flower bat makes it look like a little pig.

A bat's body is covered in silky fur. There are more than a million fine hairs on each square inch of a bat's skin. Some bats have tails that resemble the tail of a mouse. Others have no tail.

The thin legs of most bats are much like a human's, except that a bat's knee bends in the opposite direction from a human knee. The legs of most bats are

The legs of most bats are so weak that they cannot stand up or walk. They use their sharp claws to hang upside-down instead.

too weak to support the weight of their bodies, so they are unable to walk. When they land on the ground, they must crawl, pulling themselves forward with their wings and pushing with their legs. The bone structure of a bat's leg means that bats can only perch upside-down. Its five-toed feet and sharp claws allow it to hang easily.

BAT WINGS

A very thin layer of flexible skin stretches over a bat's legs, arms, and long fingers to form its wings. A flying bat can quickly change the shape of its wings by moving its fingers individually—just as you can change the shape of your hand by moving your thumb or fingers. The legs and arms of a bat are lightweight, so it is easier for the animal to fly. In some bats, a tail provides lift and helps the bat navigate.

Bat wings are different from those of birds. A bird in flight is powered by two pairs of breast muscles—one set is used for the downstroke and the other for the upstroke. In bats, the downstroke propels the animal forward. This downstroke is powered by three sets of breast muscles. Three similar pairs of muscles on the bat's back lift the wings upward.

Bats can roll to one side by changing the angle of their wings. To change direction, a bat does what you would do if you were rowing a boat. If you wanted the boat to go straight ahead, you would simply row both oars at the same rate. But if you wanted to turn left, you would row the oar on your left more quickly than the oar on your right. Similarly, a bat turns its body by beating one wing faster than the other.

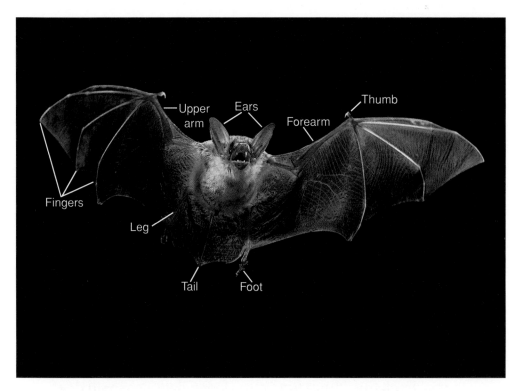

Thin flexible skin stretched over a bat's legs, arms, and fingers forms its wings. A flying bat can change the shape of its wings by moving its fingers individually.

The shape and size of a bat's wings are important. Small bats with broad wings have greater maneuverability, while species with narrower wings are capable of faster flight. Some of the larger bats, such as the greater mastiff bat, roost high above the ground and begin flight their with a free fall. This helps them pick up speed before they start horizontal flight.

Bat wings have other uses besides flight. Many insect-eating bats use their wings to catch prey. Others use their wings in mating displays. The male epauletted bat, for example, fans its wings rapidly, puffs out its cheek pouches, and makes gonglike calls to attract a mate.

MICROBATS AND MEGABATS

Bats are divided into two main groups—about 700 species of microbats and 200 species of megabats. Most microbats are smaller than megabats, but a few microbats have wingspans of more than 36 inches (90 cm). Similarly, some megabats weigh less than a ballpoint pen.

The microbats are among the smallest mammals on Earth. The Philippine bamboo bat has a wingspan of 6 inches (15 cm) and weighs little more than a paper clip. The bumblebee bat of Thailand weighs less than a penny. By contrast, the largest megabat—the flying fox—has a wingspan of almost 6 feet (2 m) and weighs 2 to 3 pounds (1 to 1.5 kg).

Flying foxes are the largest megabats. Some, like this Indian fruit bat, weigh 2 to 3 pounds (1 to 1.5 kg).

Microbats have small eyes, highly developed ears, and a remarkable ability to *echolocate*. They emit high-pitched sounds and use the returning echoes to determine the size and position of objects around them.

Microbats are found all over the world. Although most eat insects, some eat fruit, nectar, fish, small mammals, or even blood. To obtain enough energy and nutrients, bats must eat at least 30 percent of their body weight each night. Most drink water by flying low over a lake or stream and dipping their mouths into the water.

Megabats have large eyes and simple ears. Most lack the ability to echolocate. They live in Asia, Africa, and Australia and eat mainly fruit, flowers, and nectar.

This fruit bat is drinking the nectar of a balsa flower.

3 FLIGHT AT NIGHT

Some small mammals, such as flying squirrels and gliding lemurs, can stretch out their bodies and glide from tree to tree, but bats are the only mammals capable of actual flight.

Weight is always a problem in flight. Because the bat has teeth, there is a concentration of weight at the front end of its body. But since a bat has a short neck, its center of gravity is located in the upper chest where its wings are attached. If the bat had a longer neck, its center of gravity would be closer to its head, and the bat would not be able to fly.

ECHOLOCATION

While birds use magnetism for navigation, many bats—especially microbats—use echolocation. A bat sends out a series of high-pitched calls. When the sound strikes objects, it bounces back toward the bat. By listening to the echoes

The high-pitched calls of the bat go out as sound waves that strike objects and then bounce back toward the bat.

This long-eared bat uses echolocation to help it find and catch moths and other insects.

of its calls, the bat is able to locate objects. Bats can detect distance, direction, and movement. Using this information, the bat builds a mental "sound map" of its environment.

All microbats produce their sounds in voice boxes. Some

megabats echolocate by using sounds they produce in other ways. The dog-faced bat, for example, makes sounds by clicking its tongue. Not all of the sounds that bats make are for echolocation. Many of their squeaks and squawks are used to communicate with other bats.

The echolocation calls that bats use are made at a very high *frequency*. Humans can hear the echolocation calls of some bats, but most of these calls are outside the range of human hearing.

Many bats fly with their mouths open when they are emitting their high-pitched, intensely loud, ultra-brief bursts of sound. Others fly with their mouths closed and make sounds through their noses.

The ears of bats vary greatly. Some are very small, while others are quite large and well developed. Most echolocating bats have a tragus or earlet in front of their ear openings. Muscles inside a bat's ear contract just before the bat makes its calls and relax in time to hear the returning echo.

As a bat echolocates, it moves its ears quickly so that it can hear the sound bouncing back from several different angles. When a bat's calls bounce back quickly, it knows the object is nearby. The longer the sound takes to return, the farther the bat is from the object.

The unusual faces of some bats contain parts that are essential to their echolocation. For example, the leaf-chinned bat has lips that relax in elaborate folds when it is roosting.

A D'Orbigny's round-eared bat has just caught a grasshopper.

But when this bat is flying, its lips spread out like a megaphone to beam sounds forward.

Bats also use their other senses to provide information about their environment. Fruit-eating bats rely heavily on their sense of smell. Some leaf-nosed bats locate frogs by listening for their croaking. D'Orbigny's round-eared bat listens for the mating calls of its favorite *prey*, the long-horned grasshopper.

Odors and glands play a role in bat behavior. Some bats live in places where the ammonia smell from their droppings is so strong it drives humans away. Smells may also help bats get back to their home roosts.

We often hear the expression, "blind as a bat," but bats aren't blind. All bats can see to varying degrees, though only in shades of black and white. They lack the light-sensitive cells that allow humans to see colors.

FLIGHT WHILE CHASING INSECTS

A bat's flight seems erratic while it is catching insects. It dives, darts, and loops about because it chases many insects at once. A bat can identify and capture an insect in just half a second and some bats catch up to fifteen fruit flies a minute. When a bat is not chasing insects, its flight path is straight or gently curved.

Some types of insects can detect a bat's ultrasonic sounds. A moth, for example, may dive to escape being

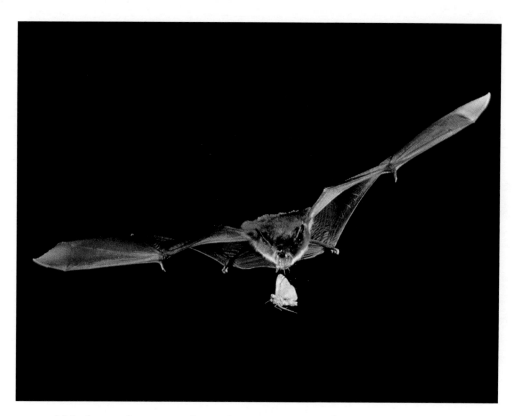

A big brown bat zeroes in on its target—a moth.

eaten. But a bat is not easily turned away from its prey. If a moth detects a bat's sounds and goes into a dive to try to escape, the bat may also dive and use its wings to trap the falling moth.

A Bat's Life 4

Some bats, like the little brown bat, choose hollows for their daytime roosts. These hollows may be in caves, mines, tree trunks, or spaces in abandoned buildings. Other bats roost in crevices in rocks or buildings, or under the loose bark of trees. The flattened skull of the South American flat-headed bat allows it to squeeze under rocks to roost.

Some bats prefer to roost in leaf litter on the forest floor. The wrinkle-faced bat uses a transparent wing membrane between its fingers to cover its eyes when roosting. This allows the bat to look out for approaching danger while hiding its eyes from predators.

These bats have made a tent-like shelter from a leaf growing in a tropical rain forest in Costa Rica.

Experiments have revealed that bats tend to return to the same roosts each day. When scientists took bats out to sea and released them, the bats returned to land and often roosted in the cave where they had originally been captured.

Spear-nosed bats often roost in large clusters.

THE WINTER MONTHS

When winter comes, life is more difficult for bats. Insects are no longer flying about in great numbers, and there is no flower nectar or fruit for them to eat. When food is not abundant, some bats *hibernate*, while others *migrate*.

Most hibernating bats seek out caves or mines where the temperature is cool and constant, usually between 40 and 48°F (4 and 9°C). Here the bats hang upside down and enter a deep *torpor*. The bats are not actually asleep, but as their body temperature falls and their bodily functions slow, they become extremely sluggish. They live on the extra fat they have stored up during the summer.

Soon after a bat settles down for the winter, its body temperature drops from about 104°F (40°C) to the temperature of the cave. Its breathing rate decreases, too. An active bat takes about 200 breaths a minute, while a hibernating bat may breathe only 23 times a minute. Even though a bat's body functions slow down, a bat that is plump when it begins its period of hibernation in the autumn will become very thin and hungry by spring.

If hibernating bats are disturbed, they wake up, their body temperature begins to rise, and they become more active. Higher levels of activity make bats burn calories more quickly. If bats are disturbed several times during hibernation, they may use up all the extra fat in their body and starve to death before spring.

A large group of bats hibernates in a rocky nook.

Many of the bats that do not hibernate, migrate. These bats fly to an area with warmer temperatures. The Mexican free-tailed bat, which lives in the southwestern United

States for most of the year, travels up to 900 miles (1,450 km) to caves in Mexico each winter.

Hoary, red, and silver-haired bats spend their summers in New York and Canada. During the autumn months, they migrate to South Carolina and other parts of the southeastern United States. In western North America, hoary bats fly from their summer range in the northwest forests to California and Mexico.

To learn more about bat migration, scientists have banded many of the guano bats that spend the summer in the Carlsbad Caverns in New Mexico. They recaptured one of the banded bats at Las Barrochas, Jalisco—810 miles (1,300 km) to the south.

A similar study of the Indiana bat showed that very few migrated any great distance. Although most did not fly south, some did travel to a winter location some 320 miles (515 km) away from their summer home.

It is hard to keep track of migrating bats because they use echolocation to avoid the nets set up to catch them. However, scientists believe that bats use the same flight paths as migrating birds.

BAT BABIES

Some bats may live up to 30 years, but their average life span is 9 to 15 years. Most female bats have one baby, or pup, each year. In temperate areas, males and females live in

This baby gray bat was born in Hubbard's Cave in Tennessee.

separate colonies until late summer when the males rejoin the females and young. In the tropics, babies are born at the beginning of the wet season when food is most plentiful.

During the mating period, male bats try to attract females in a variety of ways. They may hang from branches, flap their wings, and honk when females fly by. Some males engage in mock fights with other males to impress the females. The crested bat of Africa draws attention to itself by raising a head crest that looks something like a peacock's crest.

Most bats mate in the autumn and give birth in the spring. Pregnant females search for a protected roosting area such as a cave or deserted barn. Soon the roosting area will become a *nursery*. Often, hundreds of female bats roost and raise their young together in what is called a *maternity colony*.

Before giving birth, the mother bat hangs upside down on a branch or other surface. When a baby bat is about to be born, the mother bat reaches up and takes hold of the branch with its thumbs. The mother bat then curves its tail forward, so that its body forms the shape of a basket. The baby bat lands in this basket when it emerges, feet first, from its mother's body.

The baby clutches the branch with its toes and begins to call as soon as its head appears. The baby bat then crawls to its mother's nipple and starts to nurse. Baby bats are fed

During mating, a male Gambian bat enfolds the female within its wings.

mother's milk until they are old enough to digest solid food. As the baby feeds, the mother bat holds the baby in its wings. The mother licks the baby clean and cuts the umbilical cord with its sharp teeth. In some species, another fe-

male bat may act as a sort of *midwife* and help with the birth.

For a few days, insect-eating bats may carry their babies when they leave their roosting site at night. But when the baby is 1 week old, the mother hangs the baby in a sheltered spot and goes out in search of food. Fruit-eating bats carry their babies with them for a much longer period. Each baby uses its hooked "baby teeth" to cling to its mother's breast.

Even though thousands of little brown bat mothers and babies may live in the same cave, mother bats have no problem locating their own young when they return from hunting. Scientists believe that body odor may help a mother bat identify her young.

Free-tailed bats do not appear to look for their own young when they return from hunting. These female bats nurse whatever babies they encounter until their milk supply runs out.

This baby fruit-eating bat, or pup, clings to its mother.

The little brown bat, shown here in flight, is the most common bat in the United States.

FINDING FOOD 5

Bats eat an incredibly wide variety of foods—flying insects, crawling creatures, fruit, pollen, frogs, fish, small animals, and even blood.

FLYING INSECT EATERS

The United States is home to thirty-nine species of insect-eating microbats. The most common of these is the little brown bat, which may eat 600 to 900 insects in just 1 hour. These small bats weigh about as much as a crayon and have a wingspan of 8 to 11 inches (20 to 27 cm). Their fur is a dull brown, and their hairless ears are usually black.

This pallid bat has caught its dinner—a grasshopper.

Little brown bats live in groups. During the day, they huddle in caves or some other type of shelter. At night they echolocate, making a high-pitched clicking sound about ten times a second. When a little brown bat spots a potential meal, it hits the insect with its wing, scoops it up with its tail, and tosses it into its mouth.

GROUND FEEDERS

Pallid bats, which eat crawling creatures, live in the western United States. They have very large ears and beautiful cream-colored fur. The pallid bat catches its prey—crickets, grasshoppers, scorpions, and small lizards—on the ground.

When a pallid bat catches a scorpion, it kills its prey with one quick bite. Then the bat may fly to a safer spot where it eats every part of the scorpion, except its tail.

FRUIT EATERS AND NECTAR DRINKERS

Flying foxes are megabats and rank among the biggest and most spectacular of the fruit bats. Some have wingspans almost 6 feet (2 m) wide. Flying foxes hang like leaves in trees and often congregate in large, noisy camps. They are found in Asia and Australia. The largest flying foxes live in the South Pacific. Because of their size, they are sometimes hunted by humans and eaten for food.

Their large eyes and keen sense of smell help flying foxes locate food. These bats like to crush ripe fruit in their

In Thailand, Lyle's flying fox bats roost in groups, so they look like fruit hanging from a tree.

mouths and spit out the seeds. The seeds often sprout up wherever they fall. In this way, bats scatter the seeds of rain-forest trees. Flying foxes eat as much as they can and then—much like a squirrel—store the rest of the fruit in cheek pouches for later.

Saussure's long-nosed bat feeds at flowers. In spring, some of these nectar-drinking bats come into the southwestern United States from Mexico. They arrive when desert plants such as agave and yucca have just finished blooming.

At night, as the bats fly down into a flower blossom to feed, pollen collects on their heads. When they fly to other

A long-nosed bat is about to get a drink of nectar from the flower of a saguaro cactus.

blossoms, they deposit some of this pollen. In this way, bats *pollinate* desert flowers and also many rain-forest plants.

Long-nosed bats pollinate several plants in the southwestern United States and Mexico, including the organ pipe and saguaro cactus. The long nose and tongue of this bat enable it to reach the nectar deep inside the blossoms. The tongue may have a brush-like tip, which is used to gather pollen.

FISH EATERS

While most bats live on either insects or fruit and nectar, some eat fish. Any fish that breaks the surface of the water is a likely target for an echolocating bat. Fish-eating bats are great hunters and can easily catch prey with their claws.

The fishing bulldog bat is a microbat found in Mexico, the West Indies, Central America, and South America. Its most striking feature is its bright-orange face. It has a wingspan of up to 20 inches (50 cm) and long, strong hind feet with sharp claws.

The fishing bulldog bat flies low over rivers, bays, and lagoons. When it spots a fish, it plunges its hind feet into the water and catches its victim with its toe claws. This bat often bites its prey into small pieces and stores them in its cheek pouches. Later, the bat hangs upside down in a safe spot and eats its fish supper.

The fishing bat uses the toe claws on its hind feet to catch fish.

A frog-eating bat is about to capture its evening meal.

FROG EATERS

In Panama, male frogs spend their evenings trying to attract females. They chirp a tune that lets the females know their exact location. When a bat flies onto the scene, however, the chirping stops. If the frogs quiet down quickly, they will be safe. If not, they will be bat food.

Some frogs are *edible*, but others are poisonous. Bats can usually distinguish one group of frogs from another by the frogs' calls, but occasionally a bat makes a mistake. When this happens, a warning system of small bumps around the bat's mouth tells the bat it is in danger, and the bat quickly drops the poisonous frog.

SMALL ANIMAL EATERS

The Asian false vampire bat has a wingspan of almost 24 inches (60 cm). It has large ears and practically no tail. The false vampire bat lives in southeast Asia and India. It eats small animals such as rodents, birds, lizards, and frogs. These bats may catch their prey in the air or pick them off cave walls.

The ghost bat also eats small animals. This bat gets its name from its white body and wings. The species of ghost bat found in Australia is white with a pale-gray back. Two other types of ghost bat live in Central and South America. One has white or cream-colored wings, while the other has translucent or whitish wings.

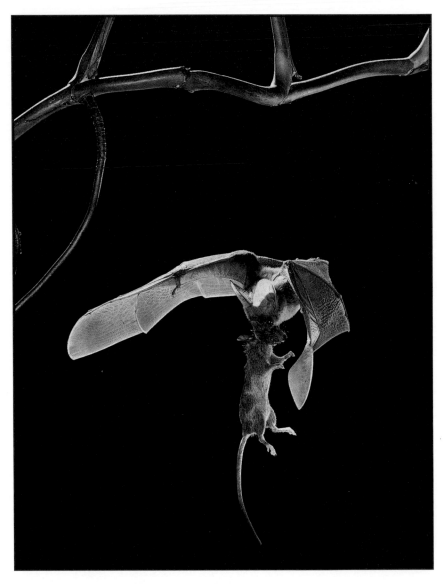

A false vampire bat hangs on tightly to its prey—a gray mouse.

BLOOD SIPPERS

Vampire bats, perhaps the best known of all bats, are found in Mexico, Central America, and South America. These bats have a tubular stomach that is specially adapted for their liquid diet of blood. Vampire bats eat no other kind of food.

This Brazilian vampire bat may look cute and cuddly, but it can be a vicious killer.

Unlike most bats, the vampire bat has strong legs. It can walk and leap like a frog in all directions.

The common vampire bat, which is grayish-brown and furry, has a wingspan of about 15 inches (38 cm). Its body is a little less than 4 inches (10 cm) long and it weighs less than 2 ounces (56 g). This vampire bat has pointed ears and no tail. Its two front teeth are long, curved, and sharp.

In the dark of night, the common vampire bat flies out to attack cattle, horses, dogs, and occasionally, humans. The bat may hover in the air and land on its victim, or it may land on the ground nearby and crawl up on the victim. Since the common vampire bat weighs so little, sleeping animals do not usually wake up when the bat lands on them.

To get its victim's blood, the common vampire bat slices the skin of the animal with its sharp front teeth. The scoop-shaped wound is usually less than 1 inch (2.5 cm) wide and about half as deep. Luckily, bats cannot bite deep enough to hit a major blood vessel.

After slitting the skin, the bat laps up blood that flows from the wound. Its grooved lip and long curved tongue, which it moves rapidly, help move the blood into its mouth. A bat may sip the blood from its victim for as long as 30 minutes. During this time, the bat drinks about 1 fluid ounce (30 ml) of blood.

Two other vampire bat species, the white-winged vampire bat and the hairy-legged vampire bat, feed mostly on the blood of birds.

This epauleted bat feeds on a ripe mango near Lake Victoria in Kenya.

FACING THE FUTURE 6

Most bats are harmless to humans, and, as you learned in the Introduction, many bats are helpful. In rain forests, they scatter fruit seeds. In many *habitats*, they are the main predators of night-flying insects. Each year, they eat hundreds of tons of insects. Without these hungry bats, these insects would destroy many of the world's crops.

Like bees, bats are also valued for their role in pollination. In Africa, bats pollinate the baobab and iroko trees. In Australia, they pollinate the hardwood forests. In the southwestern United States, bats pollinate cactuses.

In Thailand, bat *guano* is mined and sold as fertilizer. The guano mines support schools and provide jobs.

BATS IN DANGER

Although most bats are gentle and useful, they have many enemies. No predator depends on bats as a regular source of food, but many predators eat bats when they can. Opossums, raccoons, skunks, weasels, minks, bobcats, rats, dogs, and even cats eat young bats that have fallen to the ground or adult bats that are sleeping. Owls, hawks, and falcons sometimes catch bats as they fly.

The most serious bat predators, however, are humans. As a result, several bat species have become extinct. In some cases, hunters kill bats for sport. In Arizona, a group of hunters shot and killed thousands of bats living in Eagle Creek Cave. Many more bats die because people often fear the darkness and any creature in it.

Many people are concerned that bats may be carrying diseases. At one time, scientists thought most bats were rabid and warned that a bat bite could infect humans and other animals. Recent research suggests, however, that very few bats—less than one-half of one percent—carry *rabies*.

During the 1960s, hundreds of thousands of bats were killed in a huge effort to prevent vampire bats from infecting Latin American livestock with rabies. In Trinidad,

Mexico, Venezuela, and Brazil, hundreds of thousands of bats were killed by poisonous gas, flamethrowers, explosives, and guns.

Beginning in 1968, ranchers caught bats in nets and smeared a gel containing a drug on the bats' backs. When these animals were released, they groomed themselves by licking the drug off their backs. Other bats in the roost helped the bats remove the gel by licking their backs. When the bats ingested the drug, they died.

Many bats are accidental victims of human activities. Some are killed by *insecticides*, chemicals that are sprayed on plants to kill insects. When bats eat insects that have ingested these chemicals, the bats are also poisoned.

Sometimes the caves where bats roost are flooded when dams are built, or when waterways are diverted by humans. Any bats living in the cave are drowned. When abandoned mines and caves are sealed off for safety reasons, bats may be trapped inside and starve to death. If bats are trapped outside, they may have difficulty finding another roosting place.

Farmers sometimes accuse bats of destroying their fruit crops. They try to save their harvest by killing all bats—not just the bats that eat fruit. In fact, scientists who have investigated farmers' complaints believe that the crops are eaten by monkeys, not bats. According to the researchers, bats eat only ripe fruit—not the green fruit that farmers normally send to market.

SAVING THE BATS

In the late 1970s, the gray bat became the first bat listed as an endangered species in the United States. Today, six bat species in the United States are considered endangered and another eighteen species are likely candidates for the endangered species list. Among the bats on the International List of Endangered Animals is the Hawaiian hoary bat, the only bat in the Hawaiian Islands.

Since bats are not as appealing as other animals to some people, it has been hard to raise money for their protection. Merlin Tuttle, a former curator of mammals at the Milwaukee Public Museum, founded Bat Conservation International (BCI) in 1982. This group has gained protection for several bat colonies. Through the efforts of conservationists, some communities have come to value the bats that keep their town free of mosquitoes and other insect pests.

In 1986, Tuttle moved BCI headquarters to Austin, Texas. This city, known as the "Bat Capital of America," is home to hundreds of thousands of bats. Many roost under bridges in the downtown area. Each night, the bats consume an estimated 27,000 pounds (12,200 kg) of insects.

Increased awareness of the bat's usefulness has allowed some efforts at protection to succeed, but serious threats remain. It would be a great loss if all bats became extinct. Their future survival depends upon spreading accurate information about these amazing upside-downers.

Many bats roost under bridges in the downtown area of Austin, Texas. Each night, these bats devour thousands of pounds of insects.

Glossary

echolocate—to send out high-pitched sounds and interpret the echo that comes back.

edible—fit to be eaten.

evolve—to gradually change over millions of years to adapt to a particular environment.

frequency—the number of times that something occurs within a given period. The frequency of a sound wave affects its pitch.

guano—the droppings left by a colony of bats.

habitat—the place where an organism lives.

hibernate—to pass the winter in a resting state.

insecticide—a chemical substance that kills insects.

mammal—an animal that has a backbone, usually has hair, nourishes its young with mother's milk, and regulates its internal body temperature.

maternity colony—a group of females of the same species that lives together and raises young together.

midwife—one who assists during birth.

migrate—to travel regularly from one place to another.

nocturnal—moving about at night.

nursery—a roost where bats leave their babies while the adults are out hunting food.

pollen—the male sex cells of green plants.

pollinate—to transfer pollen from the anther (male part of the flower) to the stigma (female part of the flower). The pollen may be carried from one flower to another by insects, birds, bats, or the wind.

prey—animals that are hunted for food by other creatures.

rabies—a deadly viral disease that is passed on by the bite of an infected animal.

species—a group of organisms that creates viable offspring when they mate.

torpor—a state of inactivity.

Resources

Books

Bash, Barbara. *Shadows of Night: The Hidden World of the Little Brown Bat*. San Francisco, CA: Sierra Club Books for Children, 1993.

Halton, Cheryl M. *Those Amazing Bats*. New York: Macmillan, 1991

Johnson, Sylvia. *Bats*. Minneapolis, MN: Lerner, 1985

Pringle, Laurence. *Batman*. New York: Charles Scribner's Sons, 1991.

Pringle, Laurence. *Vampire Bats*. New York: William Morrow and Company, 1982.

Stuart, Dee. *Bats: Mysterious Flyers of the Night*. Minneapolis, MN: Carolrhoda Books, 1994.

Organization

Bat Conservation International, P.O. Box 162603, Austin, Texas 78716. This group prints a 16-page color illustrated booklet, *Bats: Gentle Friends, Essential Allies*. For a contribution of any amount, they will send a copy of the *Bat House Builder's Handbook*.

INTERNET SITES

Due to the changeable nature of the Internet, sites appear and disappear very quickly. These resources offered useful information on bats at the time of publication.

Bats Bats Bats provides general information about bats and includes an extensive listing of books, guides, and activity workbooks about bats. It's address is: **http://www.a-two-z.com/page_b.html**

Bats and Public Health Concerns describes fact and fiction about the diseases that can be transmitted by bats. The address for this site is: **http://www.batcon.org/fofbph.html**

Bats Shouldn't Be Pests provides information about the beneficial characteristics of bats, especially little brown bats. You can reach this site at: **http://groupweb.com/eco/bats.htm**

Conservation of Bats includes general information about bats and discusses why some bats are endangered species. It's address is: **http://www.jaguarpaw.com/BatsCon.html**

Pam's Bat Page has general information about bats and lists a number of useful links to other sites. It's address is: **http://www.viagrafix.com/pingle/bats.htm**

INDEX

ABOUT THE AUTHOR

Phyllis J. Perry has worked as an elementary schoolteacher and principal and has written two dozen books for teachers and young people. Her most recent books for Franklin Watts include *Hide and Seek: Creatures in Camouflage*, *Armor to Venom: Animal Defenses*, *The Crocodilians: Reminders of the Age of Dinosaurs*, and *The Snow Cats*. She did her undergraduate work at the University of California, Berkeley, and received her doctorate in Curriculum and Instruction from the University of Colorado. Dr. Perry lives with her husband, David, in Boulder, Colorado.